Green Pets

by Isabel Thomas

OXFORD
UNIVERSITY PRESS

Part of the Family

Pets can help people stay fit and happy. They can feel like part of the family.

Pets can help people feel less lonely, too.

Looking After Pets

Just like you, pets need:

- exercise
- toys
- food
- water.

Many things pets need are made from plastic. Plastics harm our planet. We need to go green!

A Need to be Green

Going green means helping the planet.

Collecting litter helps keep the planet green.

Pets cannot decide what is green.
We must help them to go green!

Think of all the things a pet needs.

How can pets have these things and be green? Read on for some tips.

Greener Walks

Pets need exercise every day.

Tips:

- Do not use the car! Walk near home.
- Clean up after a dog.
- Take rubbish home.

Protecting All Animals

Some cats like to exercise outside. They enjoy **prowling** around. Sometimes they look for birds.

We can help protect birds. Make a **perch** for birds to feed safely.

A bell tells birds if a cat is near.

Greener Toys

Just like you, pets enjoy playing with toys.

Tips:

- Check new toys are not made from plastic.
- Check they do not fall apart.

Turn a box into a pet's play zone.
You can hide dried treats in a card tube.

All toys must be safe for pets. Talk to your vet about the best toys to pick.

Greener Treats

Pets like to eat treats! Treats often come in plastic packets.

Plastic litter is a problem for the planet.

Homemade pet treats are greener. You can bake treats for dogs to eat.

mix

cut

bake

Treats need to be safe for pets.
Always check with an adult.

Green Pets

Greener pets help keep the planet green.

Can you think of ways to help pets be greener?

Look It Up

perch: something for a bird to rest on

prowling: creeping and looking for something

tube: long and round object

Index